Rhapsody

with

Dark Matter

~~Jeff Gundy~~

Jeff Gundy

Working Lives Series
Bottom Dog Press
Huron, Ohio

Acknowledgments

My thanks to the editors who first published these poems, some in different versions:

Artful Dodge: "Hunger," "Lemons," "White River"; *Brevity* (on-line): "Breakfast at the County Seat Café"; *Beloit Poetry Journal*: "The Sadness of Water and Women," "What the Boy Knows," "What the Old Man Says"; *Chili Verde Review*: "Other Gods"; *Cincinnati Poetry Review*: "Driving West on Easter"; *Conrad Grebel Review*: "The Little Clerk," "Driving with Rumi"; *Gospel Herald*: "Letter to Dean Scrawled Inside His New Book"; *Grand Lake Review*: "Cruise," "Gravity" ; *The Heartlands Today*: "Many Strong Rivers: Words on the Way Home"; *Kairos*: "Old Water"; *Laurel Review*: "How the Boy Jesus Resisted Taking Out the Trash," "On the Bus"; *Mennonite Life*: "The Black Father"; *Mennonot*: "Ancient Themes #1: The Martyrs & the Child": *Mid-American Review*: "The Hunter," "Right Here, or the Realist Aesthetic," "What the Prairie Boy Learned on the Whistler Road," "Life Study with Obstinate Questionings, or the Sweat Bee"; *Poet Lore:* "Braid"; *Poetry Northwest*: "Rain"; *Rhubarb:* "Valley, Old Man, Paper Cup"; *Shenandoah*: "Rhapsody with Dark Matter"; *Southern Indiana Review*: "Girls," "Late Ode"; *Snowapple*: "Day with Ducks, Sun, Eyes"; *Spoon River Poetry Review*: "Crow," "Jacob's Creek" (as "Laurel River"); *Trading Places*: "Views of the Late-Rising Moon"; *Whetstone*: "Sulfur," "Things of No Use in the Morning"; *Whiskey Island*: "Landscape with Daily Life"

"Grass" appeared in *Greeting the Dawn: An Anthology of New Mennonite Writing* (Pinchpenny Press, 1998). "Rain" appeared in *Illinois Voices: An Anthology of Twentieth-Century Poetry from Illinois* (Univ. of Illinois Press, 2000).

Thanks to the Ohio Arts Council and Bluffton College for grants and a sabbatical which made work on some of these poems possible.

For friendship and advice on these poems I am especially grateful to Jean Janzen, Keith Ratzlaff, Kevin Stein, Clint McCown, and Julia Kasdorf. And for living with me and lighting up the world, thanks to Nathan, Ben, Joel, and most of all Marlyce.

Contents

1.

Rain

And a stray face spins me back to the black-haired girl
I saw long ago and stood helpless
watching her pass, bareheaded in the rain,
the easy way she found, wet but not hunched
against it, hair damp and shining on her brow,
her shoulders. I wanted to give something
for the dark rain of that hair,
the quiet of her face, not angry or restless,
alert to each step, the crowded sidewalk . . .
But what? Words? Dark rain. Wet face.

She never saw me. We've tramped on down
our own dark tunnels now for years. What hapless watcher
at my gates would know her face, would let her in
without the password, find her a bed, say rest,
sleep, I'll be outside?

I know. It shouldn't matter
who's lovely in the rain and who isn't.
But it's not beauty or nostalgia or even lust
that's got me, I don't know what it is,
justice maybe, prisons and churches, the glowing creatures
in the center of the sun. Most days I think
I'm almost free, I don't miss a single meeting,
I don't hit squirrels with my bike. Most days
it doesn't rain, and nobody walks the streets
in black hair, a light jacket and a glaze
of shining water, rain beading and touching her
all over like the hand of someone very large
and very gentle, very far away.

Rain = sign of black matter

Hunger

"For this I have abandoned all my other lives."
-Robert Francis, "Waxwings"

Who could argue from this broad front porch in Camp Hill,
Pennsylvania, the mountain across the way, primrose blooming
just a day after snow, doves and sparrows in the trees

and Julia looking out to see if I'm hungry. I say no
just because it's so fine here with the cardinals chasing
and chirping for love or territory, the smart things

I might have said this afternoon, the sawdust from upstairs
where David is fixing bookshelves. They've been living here a week.
I can't stay past tomorrow but for now I'm not moving.

Last night we talked too late. This morning we packed books
from the basement, saving only the best ones, Jackie and Lee
in Europe, a colored sketch of brave Teddy Roosevelt

watching the lion maul a hapless native. Hunger and territory.
Guns and love. The air above the mountain is complete,
invisible, impure. My head feels hard and light

as those puffy mints that collapse on your tongue.
The writer insisted we can't say, "That table isn't there."
God either. Or the porch. Can we say where we stand

in the world, in anybody's heart, in the foamy eyes of God?
There's sun on the mountain, a city between it and me.
Yes, I'm hungry. I eat and eat and never does it last.

On the Bus

The bus was 2/3 empty, quiet, when I glimpsed blond hair
in the next row up, a white sleeve, red fingernails.

How couldn't I look when her homely, buzz-cut boyfriend
just looked at her too, coolly, miles at a time.

They didn't talk much. Two years, I figured, she'd be married
and miserable, tending this flatbrained skinhead's kid.

He'll drink, be jealous, hit her. She'll leave almost too late.
I was ready to stop him right there when we arrived

in Evansville and they stood up and hugged. She went off
to find her luggage. They had just met on the bus, were only

flirting a little, passing the time. My kids would say, duh.

I stood near her on the concrete. He was gone. She carried
a long umbrella, spoke so calmly, not to me. I wouldn't know

her face today. My life's too full. She's gone, the bus
is gone, I'm paddling like a dog in this swamp of greedy moves

and sloppy wishes. I wanted to give her something, some cheap
blessing. What does it mean, to give, to have? I never said

a word to her, and now she's almost here. Almost. Desire
has no end, no bottom, no use. It's not the way you think,

I'm just a little greedy, I want her and all that beauty
to be holy and be mine and still her own, like a mountain

we leave off the maps, a lake we talk about only in whispers.
I want her to tell me I'm the one, forever. I want her

to break me, heart and health. I want to wear her down
to powder. I want to yearn forty years and die splendidly.

I want never to see her again.

Lemons

And it didn't snow yet, though they promised. And on the distant coast a woman arrived at Emergency with an alien sheen on her body, flecks of white and yellow floating in her blood, and she vomited and died there, and a nurse and doctor went down too. We're still inquiring. We're troubled.

All week I've felt vague and distracted, a little sore throat but that's not it. What are these phrases that push up and then die like mushrooms? If the sidewalks didn't fill like ditches in the rainy season, if ice and black sand didn't grate on me so, I could be happy here. I could get something done.

If I lived on the coast, where the pale walls glowed weirdly as her body found its final, enigmatic twist. If I knew the cancer was at the bone and no God had stepped forth to save my body or my mind. If I lived in Carmel on the blazing shore or Sausalito on the shining hill and rose in winter to bird song and flowers—would the cool jade carvings of the mountain and the temple speak to me then? Would I still take any glimpse of beauty and shame as the sly work of God?

If I lived in California I'd pick oranges today, I'd groan for the lemons rotting on the ground, I'd haul the best ones down to church and find some one to need them, some woman with an odd glow who will show up unannounced and unremembered in a haze of ammonia and need, her blood flecked white and yellow as though she'd mainlined lemons and oranges, craved the great sweet juice of the western shelf, the blood and the navel, the sun going out in the ocean to drown itself again.

The Hunter

On the ice, stumpy geese stand around, trying
to look like plaster geese. Comfort and joy
have many names. *When the sun came out*

I decided to frolic, Sherri told me,
damn all the books. The duck squawks
like a man squawking like a duck. So many

messages. *The pain is exquisite,* Abbie
wrote, *I know exactly where it comes from.*
With me it's just the thought of the head-on,

the impossible crunch and the hollow beyond.
Not even a temptation, just a chance
I know is there, like those questions

my bitter friends ask: wouldn't you shoot
a man to save your wife? Would you chew
your foot off like a fox? In the book

about the fox some bastard hunter
blasted him all over the last page
and I was angry—not with the hunter,

with the story. Snow melt drips
and the planet spins and at
the quarry's edge the surface shivers,

the rest just waits. Every bare tree
trails out its slippery ends. Geese
and ducks flap and tatter in the sun

and old stories soften in the open water.

Breakfast at the County Seat Café

Someone turned the house into two dining rooms with the kitchen between, this smallish one crammed with the end of the morning rush, construction guys fueling their achy get-it-done bodies, older men in no special hurry, waitresses bustling among us all. The only space is at the counter right next to the register, last place I'd choose—I always want my back to a wall.

But the grandmotherly waitress talks to me, brings more bad coffee than I want, and I tune in to the hum and buzz and feel all right. The eggs are big and cooked just so and I eat the first piece of toast with them and the second with the blackberry jam.

The guys stroll up to pay their $3.94 or 68 cents for just coffee and maybe they notice me and maybe not but it's safe as churches, I know I can say no thanks next time the coffee comes around, I can pay and get out the door before my stomach muscles clench entirely with caffeine and the familiar strangeness of life a hundred miles from home at the County Seat Café.

When the rush slacks off the waitresses wash and dry, talk about another woman, the mall, some story. "She thinks I'm telling stories? She knows more about me than I know about her!" "That's right!" "I don't know anything about her!" That's right.

I love the hidden hollows inside rooms, inside language. I love to sit like a rock in the stream and wonder at the burbling around me. I love the exclamation mark, the dash, the waitresses bumping hips as they crowd past each other with plates of eggs and sausage. I love that half-laugh, the worlds inside it, the coins swept off the counter and the near-clean rag behind, yellow gloves and bruises at the hip and thigh, one more morning of men who need food and coffee and talk and are willing and able to pay.

Late Ode

(after Horace)

Oh let it go, honey. We won't know
what Jesus has marked out for us until
the gimpy end of time, anyway.
Put the damn self-help books away.
Maybe we'll totter off into the dark
like old Kermit and Velma across the street,
me putting on your shoes, you mine.
Maybe we won't last out this winter
as the wind yanks at the old chimney
and sand from the mortar sprinkles the snow.
We won't be young tomorrow, but odds are
we won't be dead either. We'll live
if the laundry sits till Monday. I'll go
to Kibbee's for a bottle, you put
the kids to bed. You can pour. We'll drink,
and talk, and grab whatever we can reach.

Girls

1.

What about the way schoolgirls scream, happily, completely, so you'd swear they would shred their voices, when they're just surprised or threatened in the midst of some meaningless, absorbing game, when they know there's no real danger. It's a light in the sunshine, a sizzle up the spine, the way those girls scream, eager and secure, and a man like me half a block away pausing to listen, wondering how they can do it. They don't need my protection or want my attention. They are fine and screaming, young and dusty with the playground dust, when the screaming is done they turn back to each other, talk fast, interrupt, listen, what should they play next? What will the teams be? Who will play the mother, the teacher, the child? Don't waver, don't get mushy, it's not romantic either. Cool your jets. Keep your distance. You think you have rights?

2.

Here's a right: to buy at an affordable price an inflatable version of *The Scream* by Edvard Munch, in one of two sizes, at various museum gift shops. Two of my friends have the large size and one the small. There it is, with its mouth stretched deep as though by Jupiter's gravity or some horrible flesh-softening chemical and its hands held to its face to hold something, barely, together, silent of course except for a gentle, involuntary sighing as it is uninflated. The painting itself is even more silent. But expressive. Something to do with W. W. II, as I recall, though I can't find the reference in my office. It's fifty years since D-Day. The papers are filled with remembrance and war. Old paratroopers land on the beaches, most of them safely. Others complain that *their* brave deeds are being slighted.

3.

What is it with those girls? So innocent they sound, so carefree, not learned, the way boys don't learn to point sticks and threaten each other, they just do it. I think they are being practiced for something they don't understand. I hope they never have to. Our oldest son's first weapon was a plastic golf club. We don't have daughters. We kept a five-year-old for some friends a few weeks ago. I held her carefully on my lap. She is smart and pretty, not shy. She was fine until Sunday night, leaving the movie, when we said that her parents wouldn't be home until late. She cried just a little and I held her, promised she could stay up and wait for them. Ten minutes on the couch and she fell asleep. I carried her upstairs in her little nightgown, quiet and warm as any little girl asleep where she almost belongs.

-for Elise

Smile

1.

In the coffee shop at the Colorado Springs Hilton I read Rilke and drank thick Starbuck's till my head whirled. "We must die because we have known them." "Do the heart-work, the looking is done." "Learn to love the woman inside." Indeed. I used to think love was easy but it's tedious and exacting, now isn't it, so easy to botch completely. Today people praised me and asked for copies and I thanked them, thinking how strange. They called me brave but I'm mainly greedy, I stand in the shower every morning and plot how to make the world love me. It will never be enough. It's plenty. *We're running a marathon*, said someone, *the table is set*.

It was good there, alone in the middle of the voices. The gates were open. The lights blinked. I drank coffee until my head was loose and sparky. My legs tensed, ready to take me somewhere. I kept them still somehow, pushed the pen across the paper, watched and listened as if the secret word was *merchandise*, or *caffeine*.

2.

Winging on over America I read more of Rilke's arcane interior cosmologies and Robert Hass's equally arcane glosses, all loss and melancholy, yearning for the irretrievable Other. Next to me two tan and healthy young women leaned over *Better Homes and Gardens*, discussing diets and decorating tips. Not a wrong life, surely. Better than mourning your firstborn, luckier than walking through the snow away from your smoking village.

In the airport I heard a voice: this is the beginning of World War III. It didn't slow anyone down. I drank bottled water, fought a headache, thought of coffee. I want so much, I want to write a ten line poem as dense as a neutron star, too heavy to move, so tightly packed it will glow with its own light. But I haven't even given up footnotes yet. How can I hope to be forgiven? The woman beside me absently stroked her perfect brown thigh. We said not a word in three hours. I hoped she was not reading this.

As her unsteady pile of cups and plates and napkins teetered I laughed a bit with her, quite a tower I said. When we shifted to get off, with no warning she gave me a brief, dazzling smile—just the smile that women learn, I suppose, especially pretty women, part defense and part weapon. I only smiled back and said nothing, but I carry it with me still, that gesture as graceful and un-earned as sun cracking through clouds.

If I walk out into the fields today it will be miles and days through cold mud to the end of my ignorance and guilt, to the lady who will hear me and smile and grant the wish that I cannot even name.

The Sadness of Water and Women

1.
How many lies can the wrens
and cardinals try

before they find
the one to save them?

Who wouldn't want to be
the favored son?

Twists of last year's grass.
The heavy water sprawled and chill.

The red and yellow swirls
the leaves will soon crawl through.

2.
Go out easy. Pick the feet up.
Breathe and wait. Is it control you need?

Some praise? A good rest? Tell a story.
Once I told a story. Once

we hugged in the hospital room
and when I left the door locked behind me.

You still don't get it. Who
gets it. Tell your fear. No, show it.

Oh no. Let's have a joke,
an anecdote, let's say how the thin clouds

tip away from darkness, how
the new shoots rub themselves awake,

how the boys yell up behind me.
My friends are all stressed, tired

or crazy but I'm OK, it's Friday,
burgers on the grill.

3.
It's easier to love each other
when the world allows it. When three girls
are dancing on the stones. When for years
you've listened to the choir
and known the highest, sweetest voice
was coming home with you.
When she says *it's just so hard
out there* and you say, where?

4.
What to do when you need a word
when all you know is the sadness of water

and women and your own guilty joy
when the quarry changes color changes shape

everywhere your eyes glance off it
when the nurse comes to say it's time

and the door clicks shut

what to do

declare survive suppose
adjust hush

forty-four degrees
the sun still lying low

the red-splashed duck churns gently off
the heron blank and sober as a sword

hauls its lanky bones at last
toward some other shore

tomorrow the women will still be sad
tomorrow the water will still be blue

Old Water

-for Julia and Ginny

If I had known, if I had known, would I ever
have thought to cross the bridge, to
shuck my clothes and slide into the quiet water?
In the fall, leaves languid on the cool lip
as the girls who'd never look at me.
Oh please . . .

When I went under what was waiting
touched me, wrist and thigh, and held firm,
strong, and settled deep with me.
I was desperate, then wild and then
my panic drifted off like an old whiff of skunk
and left the new stars dazzling, scent
of oniongrass and violets, the shape below me,
warm and smooth, the body nestled
inside the intimate water.
You could be so free, it whispered.
You could be so good.
I could not speak—and yet
I said, *Not this way.* I said
Not this time. What did I mean?
I could barely think of apples and children,
another life, and then the voice . . . *All right.*
All right. You won't go far.
                              Do I remember
after that? Mud, the hard sticks,
light splayed along the surface. Damp clothes
and my hands among them. Then traffic
and trees and this step, that step, thin
rusty slats of the stairs leading down.

So it's all about God, is it, or else not,
or else it's me and the stream I yearn toward
day and night, hour and year,
the stream I can hear and almost see
as two lovely women swing past
on the other trail.
They do not see me
and I let them go. But oh,
the beautiful saunter
of those women deep in their talk.
They walk the path up the mountain
and the old, old water tumbles down,
tumbles down.

Day with Ducks, Sun, Eyes

First sultry day, ducks
in shiny pairs on the lawns
of Lawn Avenue, too stunned
by lust and sunshine to care
who grabs and wrings their lustrous necks.

A thousand years ago a man
named Ibn al-Haytham observed
*If we look too long at the sun
our eyes burn*, never mind how long
or loud how many experts say otherwise—
if we look too long
at the sun
our eyes burn.

And I can almost believe that desire
enters us from outside as light does
almost believe with Augustine
that the world is a riddle God invented
to force us to ponder the next world—

why else this morning
as I lay with my faithful sweetie
did I open my eyes
to her face her eyes
when a thousand times
I have closed them?

What passed between us
beyond the familiar touch of bodies
stunned and alerted me

whose eyes should be burned black
from staring into the suns.

This new world
what is it?
Pale beach, hills behind,
the hard oaks, the meadows ablaze—
oh, the sun begins everything.
But we are not the end.

Sun = desire — comes thru
eyes = ducks overcome
w/ desire

Rhapsody with Dark Matter

What's moving on the hills could be mist or rain
the first long notes of the apocalypse

or just another load of thick summer dreams.
What's coming won't be hurried or put off.

Yes the stars are out there, blazing, and all
the dark matter too. A woman with son and daughter

settles in beneath a bridge, smooths cardboard
with a dirty hand. A man pours beer and brags

of the tank he drove into the desert. Two million bucks.
So much easier to blow things up than get them right,

a marriage, a country, a small town forty miles
from the nearest beer. It isn't just this poem

that's loose, gliding from scenery to disaster,
floating through the gorgeous, deadly world.

It's not just me. Say what you will about the dark—
it won't leave you contented, or alone. It saunters

at its own pace down the long bluff, up the streets
of the finest little town in Arkansas. I'm trying

to remember where the keys are, which road I'll take
out of town. Remembering a voice: *I'm tired, yes.*

The boys are fine. Call Tuesday. Bring yourself home.

2.

Many Strong Rivers: Words on the Way Home

1.

I've got the Streets of Gold Gospel Hour on the radio, I'm cruising along through northeast Arkansas, a little mist above the rivers but not enough to slow me down. I've seen an armadillo on the road, dead, I've seen a beautiful wildflower garden and in the same moment had a bird curl out and into my headlight, so that I heard the thunk and saw it on the road behind me. It's a beautiful morning.

I've crossed the White River, running fast and clear, twice in this first hour of my way home from the workshop. I crossed four of what must be irrigation canals, one right next to the other, running perfectly straight from northeast to southwest like someone took a big four-toothed comb to the earth. They must go to the Mississippi. They struck me as beautiful, too, in a very odd and formal sort of way.

I've been thinking about paths to the sacred, ways of approaching it. I've just heard Linda Gregg talk in her startlingly resonant and clear-headed way about seeking the sacred through romantic love, through sexual love, her conscious, passionate pursuit of the kind of relationship to another human being that could somehow remain in a state of permanent ecstasy, although she knows well the odds against that quest. Being a practical guy myself, and boringly monogamous for too many years to count, I have my own doubts. But that vision of some ultimate affair, of a relationship that would not slide into gentle, enduring love but stay at the first, white heat of initial passion forever . . . who can think of that and not yearn, some way? Who can hear lines like these and not yearn?

> Taken as an animal, she yields
> to that desire which devours.
> Happy in yielding her body
> to the other who wants this altering,
> the darkness he pushes her through.

The two of them lost but alive
in the land of death on fire.
("We Do This with Our Bodies," *The Sacraments of Desire*)

Hearing Gregg read poems like this one, and talk a little about her life, I had the thought that people like her are in the world either so that people like me don't have to live that way, or because people like me don't get to live that way. I wasn't sure which. I'm not yet.

On the other hand, I'm thinking of Jack Gilbert's poem "The Abnormal Is Not Courage," which turns away from the idea of brilliant gestures, toward the celebration of various sorts of sustained accomplishment, things that build over a long time:

Not the Prodigal Son, nor Faustus. But Penelope.
The thing steady and clear. Then the crescendo.
The real form. The culmination. And the exceeding.
Not the surprise. The amazed understanding. The marriage,
not the month's rapture. Not the exception. The beauty
that is of many days. Steady and clear.
It is the normal excellence, of long accomplishment.
(*Monolithos: Poems, 1962 and 1982*)

2.

What I think at first is road kill, and something big, a deer maybe, is just some hay fallen from a truck, what looks like a whole bale. As I go by I scatter it a little more, and everyone that goes by scatters it a little more. And right afterwards I come up behind a semi piled high with great big round bales, wisps of hay pulling loose and streaming off into the wind, scattering back like some stringy greenish rain, all the way down the road.

And that's just before I come to the Mississippi . . . "I do not know much about gods, but I think the river is a strong brown god." That was Eliot, of course, who never trusted the body or romantic love either one, but grew up in St. Louis, hard by the strong brown god. There are many rivers in this part of the world, many strong rivers. They run fast and deep.

Here's an idea, a hope: that living an everyday, frazzled, even frantic life like mine can also be a kind of spiritual discipline, a way of searching for the sacred and recognizing or seizing upon or opening yourself to it when it finds you in the midst of it all. And that in fact the sacred will find you in the midst of that life, if you can somehow manage the right stance toward it.

Well. I'm brooding on desire, on what chance there is of living in both the spirit and the flesh, and also brooding about whether I should rotate my tires.

Is it possible to recognize that your desire will never be satisfied, and come to terms with that, without becoming merely bitter or merely resigned?

3.
Trying to learn the gods. Trying to learn what it means to worship. What else is worth doing?

Why did the troubadours write about women that they barely touched, or never touched? Maybe that was the only safe way. Maybe they knew that to touch, to take, to give yourself to the beloved is always to start down a road, and that all roads lead somewhere. Maybe they knew that not to touch meant never to take the road, only to look down it, and that looking down the road it does not seem to end.

What gets put into your shadow when you don't act on your desires? What gets put into your shadow when you do?

4.
Here it is, here it is, Linda. Heaven, that's where romantic love will be unending, immortal. In heaven the lovers never part. In heaven the lovers never tire. They never go off to the bathroom . . . In heaven the lovers truly learn God through bodies, in bodies, and they remember everything they learn, so there is always another thing to learn. On earth we learn God too, but forget every time, we cannot make ourselves remember, and so we must learn the same thing over again and again, having forgotten, and it is only the first thing.

And then I remember a verse from Jeremiah. I heard a beautiful sermon preached on it long ago, by a man who resigned his position a few years later, admitting that his passions had taken him beyond what the church could allow in its servants. "Seek the peace of the city where I have sent you into exile, and pray to the Lord on its behalf, for in its peace you will find your peace."

5.

And so I spend the morning cruising across America, feeling like the designated mind of God, desire and beauty and hope churning in my head until I'm dazed by more than the driving. I stop at a McDonalds somewhere and order the special of the month, what they call a hero burger, and sit down and watch the family across from me. There's a half-bald, quick-eyed guy in his thirties— he looks alert, not smart but alert. And a dark-haired, slightly heavy woman with him, a baby on her shoulder. She holds the child until it's time for her to eat and then gives him to the other woman who is with them, a grandmother I suppose. What kinds of desire go around in their heads? What would they say if I asked them?

Two young women sit down behind me and one says to the other one, "Do you think they'll ever get back together?" I can't hear the answer, but I hear her starting to explain, and I know it will take all through lunch. What are we doing in this world?

I'm sucking coffee from my cup until my lip is sore. Trying not to say things into the tape recorder. This is getting too long.

6.

What do desire and the will have to do with each other? In five minutes I go from sunshine to a downpour, not because of anything I wanted, except to go along this road.

My people have always thought, always hoped, that if you wanted to bad enough, and had Jesus to help, it would be possible to be good, possible to make your desire flow within the banks if not to dam it up forever. And there's no denying that for some of them it's worked, or almost worked. And there's no saying what's been lost, or how much. Where do we get the idea that we are in control of anything? This may be the year, Thoreau says, that the water will rise within us, and drown all our muskrats.

The rain has stopped almost as fast as it began. Linda, your poems and the work you've set for yourself seem to me beautiful and true and dangerous, as everything that's beautiful and true is dangerous. What I really want to do is thank you. And to know more. And to see God as plain as the hills of Kentucky and as permanent as the hazy sky. And more. And more.

And an old white van crouches by the off ramp with its engine irrevocably blown, surrounded in gray, oily smoke, like a huge, dirty cotton ball with a rock at the center. How quickly disaster finds us.

7.

These are the Kentucky hills, so beautiful. How little I see of them even when I remember to look, how fast they go by, how much I miss. This is the body of the world. This is the trace, the dwelling of God, of the gods. Desire is the woven body of the world, there in every tree, every blade of grass, every wildflower and crushed armadillo. Here is the world, and here we are in it like pebbles so small we blow in the wind, like shards of cooking pots broken centuries ago. And here we are going around, going around, thinking, dreaming, calling out, demanding to know about desire.

It's yearning that's eternal. Consummation is mortal.

I'm tired enough, I crave the bitterness enough, that this coffee tastes good even when it's almost cold, almost gone.

3.

Driving West on Easter

1.
What does it take to make the trip? I'd be happy for a sign, a note, the voice of God. The sign I have says route 30, Buettner Road. On a white barn, shadow cutouts, waving man and woman, jumping dog, cheerful as television. Three thin girls in Wolcott, walking, smoking, smiling. Me in my white car, unobserved, wanting every leaf to be a bird, every bird an angel. Something in the ditch—a dingy paper, filled with wind.

2.
A man needs to dream, even if it's hard as passing on route 24, risky as writing in this notebook propped on the steering wheel, the jerk of adrenalin as tons of metal loom inches from my cherished flesh. Stupid, I know, but what would you do, the absolute quick hum leaks in at every seam, the final whisper drums in the winds of passage, the engine murmurs now, now. On the overpass: I love you Jeff. Just like that.

3.
South of Gridley, a quarter-section remnant of prairie, charred yesterday by a sweaty white-haired man whose picture made the paper, dragging a fire broom, spreading flames, hurrying carefully, explaining the centuries of practice on his side. I love that picture, I want to drag a fire broom over my prairies, run beside the clean flames, watch the dainty shoots sniff into the sunlight. But here the smoke has cleared, it's a blue still Easter in the Mackinaw Breaks, yellow branches, red branches, making their beautiful empty moves.

4.
Two hours 46 minutes to St. Louis, the bridge over the strong brown god. I sweep down a long hill into the Loutre River valley, buds swelling, nets of yellow, green, red, caught in the small trees. How big the world is. How hard to keep it in my head.

5.

And I know what binds me, sends me cruising toward Emporia on new black-top, the swerves and maneuvers that have me driving west on Easter. No simple life. No blazing sign. Moments when the traffic thins, the road arrows to the west, the sun makes another run on the warm skin of the world. These words, just rehearsals for the great day when the glowing vowels will stretch from cup to wine, from chapter to verse, all along the roaring stone and flesh and wind and fire that is me and you and the Mongol hordes and the secret lives in the Marianas Trench, the world that climbs and spins in the Kansas evening, calm and still and moving as Easter in a car alone, six hundred miles behind me and a dozen to go, twelve miles to Newton and the house of the stranger who asked me to come, so far, so good, where the guest room is ready when I knock on the door.

Cargo

There must be a lighter way. I walked into the night,
restless when I should have been tired. I walked
to the waterfall but two men in white shirts

were there, moving, talking. I walked along the river
until the darkness stopped me. No, not the darkness
but what I saw within it, the vaguest glimmer,

the haziest body in the space between trees.
I waited and stepped toward it and it slid ahead.
Again. Then I knew it was light from the last cabin

slipped through branches, caught above the rocky trail.
Men were still out, hauling sleeping bags inside,
truck tires crunching on gravel. It wasn't so late,

though I should have been tired. I should have walked on.
I wanted to think I was lonely and clear, that it was late
as well as dark and I was ready to wax sadly tuneful

on the mercy and wisdom of the complicated night,
the river and its nearly human song, the road behind
with its trucks and souls and bodies moving

down the blinding tunnels like driftwood or cargo,
the hot stars above and all the radios on.

Braid

How perfectly my shadow leads me down
the path, how well it shows
the arm that flaps too much, the creaky knee.
How long till I get any of this right?

How many runs before the three white dogs
stop barking as I pass?
When one comes at me, dragging its chain,
what can I drop behind to buy some time?

There's plenty of time. Benjamin said
it isn't empty: every second is the strait gate
the Messiah might just saunter through.
If you can't hear the creaking, don't blame me.

Remember Beethoven in the last years,
snarling at visitors, sawing the piano legs
off at the hip. There are many princes,
he said, but only one Beethoven.

Here the water lies restless, not dreaming,
here the clean birds lift themselves away.
Ends and means and beginnings
weave themselves close, a braid down the back.

We could shut down tomorrow.
We could clap hands and rise.
For us, said Benjamin,
in this quick moment time has stopped.

Still the road bends and I curl with it
and the shadow leans deeper
into the quiet earth, not lost,
but harder to see.

Sulfur

-after reading James Dickey, *To the White Sea*

A still, cold day. Even the vapors from the sewer plant seem purified, freed and cleaned by the winter sun. But it's only the breeze, drifting the thick hydrogen sulfide north instead of west. Ducks and geese squawk on the quarry, a small mammal rustles in the brush.

I'm no hunter. I can barely tell cat tracks from rabbit. I don't even favor hawks over people, though I think I understand why Jeffers did, though I read straight through James Dickey's book about the gunner who gets shot down over Tokyo and walks all the way to Hokkaido, killing geese for down to make quilted pants, killing people for shoes and needles.

Beneath the hot action and the stylish prose I thought I could feel something else, a yearning to slide cold and silent through the world, to live and kill alone like a marten or a hawk, not a breath or bullet wasted. I read on, tense, stunned, merciless. The words went hazy, smelled more than seen, like game scent on a southern breeze, like sulfur on an open road.

The man wins through to the northern island, to a life so chilled and simple that when the soldiers come at last he thinks the bullets are passing right through. He thinks his great secret trek through the cold and the enemy's country will live forever, the hawk dropping soft and sharp on a rabbit, a mouse, the hot blood in the snow.

And I cannot say what is left in the space at the end of the last page, in the white cold place where body and story freeze and disappear. The words were light and strong as feathers. I cannot say what it is that lasts, that rises.

Cruise

I'm driving the curves and twists of route 6, 10:18 pm. Drizzle, my wipers whanging back and forth, trucks throwing big sheets of smeary water. It's a beautiful night, a beautiful night.

The little factory's doors are wide open and they're loading trucks at ten on a Thursday night. Down the road the porch light blares in a stone entryway, lighting up everything in welcome or fear.

There's music in the raindrops but the scale's so delicate that it takes better ears than mine to hear it, a better head than mine to get the tune.

What is better than the way a voice can take a simple string of words and tune them up, find a music that you'd never think was there. Sweet notes from the beat-up Martin fade slowly into the road noise.

The cruise control does this weird surging thing and I don't know why. I just want to get home. It's good to make the four lane highway, it's good to have some space to move so fast when you don't know who's in the other car and don't much trust yourself.

And the truth is the Indigo Girls are done and Emmy Lou is into "When the Trumpet Sounds," her voice clean and true and the guitars floating airy and hot and angelic behind and the rain almost seems to have stopped and the pavement almost seems dry.

And what could be a light or a whole new space blossoms out between the ground and the clouds ahead, a wide orange glow and of course it's the lights of Fort Wayne and a hundred thousand of us swirling all around on the surface of the earth, nothing so special, unless it's you.

And was I just awe-struck, was I just frozen, was I just taken, was I just awakened. Was I just heading steady, steady, steady down the road.

When the rain stops it's as though the world makes sense. When the rain stops I'm ready to quit worrying that these cars are filled with drunks and dopers, splashing through the dark when all the good folk are in with their feet up, glasses in their hands, watching, watching whatever's on.

When the rain stops it seems I know what I'm doing. It seems I'm almost ready to wrestle this ghostly measure into something real, start it off and let it move, casual, triumphant, nothing so special unless it is happening to you.

Letter to Dean Scrawled Inside His New Book

"I know it would be best if I didn't
say anything about God."
                    -Dean Young, *Strike Anywhere*

Jeez, Dean, twenty years almost since you turned up
in Bloomington like a hungry crow. You'd drag out some
ragged Frank O'Hara poem, and Look, you'd say, just look.

You can still make me laugh and look, realize how hip
I'll never be. If you were here now . . . Tonight
I walked to the video store with Ben, and the church

was full of people coming for the big choir concert,
the rest of town heading to the high school gym
where the girls could be undefeated if their best player

hadn't blown her ACL. We checked out "Outbreak" and
"Fearless" and when Marlyce got home we caught her up
on the whole plot even as Dustin Hoffman was saving

his ex-wife, a small California town, and the entire U.S.A.
The other boys are off somewhere, who knows. "No man lives
his life for himself," Ralph Ellison said. Children, wives,

intestinal parasites—you know the list. Greedy as I am,
I know he's onto something. A few more years here
and I'll start to think this is normal, even without graffiti

or a place to sell plasma. Even church. God is all over
towns like this one, casting a slippery weird light on
the streets and siding. Despite the "Christian" coalition

and self-righteous letters in the paper, the church folk
are mainly less obnoxious than the hoods, the guys who call
my kids soccer fags, and the town council. Next to

the professors, the preachers read more than anybody in town.
"There's so much spirit-stuff in this world . . ." says
your poem that somehow I turned to right away, packed

with the yearning and leaning I know and love, and maybe
some of your friends are laughing but not me, Dean, not me.
I can't prove there's a next world either. I can't prove anything.

But I think it's good to sing, to hear the stately old verses
read right out loud. It's good afterwards to stand around
and talk about crops or soccer or any damn thing. These days

the old men grab me by the arm and say they read my book,
they remember my great-grandpa or my great-uncle Don,
a big man on campus in 1938. They tell me stories, they say

"Keep it up!" until I can't stand it and slip out the door
and down the alley past the grade school, past the bell
that called the children of Bluffton to school till 1948,

which is perched now on a pad of brick and concrete with
a bronze plaque. The kids climb on and make it bong, bong
in its hollow and foggy way, as though it's back in its

vanished tower, still calling the children to come inside.

Gravity

It's the beautiful necessity, everything I hate and need desperately. Yes I'll tell all. Yes radiance and grief will contend. Yes the keyboard is planted firmly on the desk, and the carpet shows no signs of loosing its earthly bonds. Yes when Rommel drove deep into Egypt the dust of his passage surely did settle back to the round and greedy globe.

This is not off the subject, which is gravity, which has got us. Lift your hand, let it fall. Consider those books solid on the shelves. Chunks of turkey fallen to the floor, dimes slipped between fingers. The chairs, the mattress, the deep earth.

How to reckon what we can't escape? As well plot weather trends lost in the white-out. As well discern the ageless features of agape tangled with your sweetie on her daddy's couch, hormones whooping like movie Indians down your hungry blood.

The policeman said to the traveler: Give it up! But both of them were really Kafka, or his father, and what did they know? The winter darkness grinds me down, but when the sun comes out it dazzles from the screen, blinding. It's all elegantly tuned to its purposes, inscrutable and vast as miles of light above the ocean.

What do we have but the suck of the world? Sunlight and words and the muscles and tubes of these fleshy hunks we ride like angry ghosts. Words are no more free than golden birds. The emperor is dead, and eternal. Long live gravity. Long live the whirring world.

The Little Clerk

Sunday morning, ten o'clock, north through the greening,
partly ruined hills. Miles of thin grass behind the sign

for the Consolidated Coal Company, no fences, nothing moving.
Then cattle in a scrubby draw, black cow calmly grazing the ditch.

In the restaurant I asked dumb questions: Do you like Chicago?
Do you have sons? We both have sons. Do you feel grief,

you asked, when you think of them? Not *about* them, *of* them?
We talk and talk, we do, and then when it matters we go slow

and awkward, hoping not to disappoint. Still you seemed to me
a brother, lost for generations. What should we need to say?

It's all trying to become nobody, you said. I hate religion.
What is the ground of language, if not prayer? This must sound crazy.

You said, You still go to church when you don't have to?
And were impressed, envious maybe. I said I'd stopped trying

to escape, I said I've only almost surrendered. In Holmes County,
crows harry the red hawks. Tourist farms loll among the strip mines.

Three young men in gray stocking caps and plain clothes pump
their bicycles up the highway towards town. We're *not* separate,

you said, we're just *not*. Now you're on a plane, I'm here
with my windows rolled tight, music and coffee and the country

rolling by like a silent movie or the set for the rest of the story,
or the suit the jailors bring for the great man to wear before

the governor. Just before they bring him in the little clerk bends
to tie his shoe. The cup on the dash basks in the sun, so clear,

the slight green flecks, the whirls of brown, the glaze webbed
and crazed, clinging hard. I pick it up, I drink the coffee, still hot

and good. I swing onto the ramp and it slides an inch, adjusting,
as though it's learned some small, precious secret, and from now on . . .

-For LYL

Views of the Late-Rising Moon

The moon low & red. A fading coal fire.

The inner provinces flinch and mutter at scenes
of scrawny children, dirty shelves, bare beds.
Fortunately we do not require their ardor.

The moon a thumbprint in the slick clay.

The trumpeter swan collapsed at the quarry edge,
a pale, oversize mystery among the common geese,
swallowed buckshot burning inside.

The moon too big, too hot, too hollow.

The thin man explained the culmination of his years
of study: that in his boundless love God calibrates
the agony of each poor soul in hell.

The moon a smudge pot, an offering.

Each sinner, he said, desires to be tormented—
each chooses eternal pain. The lean face shone
with conviction. Our God, he said, only provides.

The moon a red doorway, a rip in the sky.

Other Gods

There are other gods, but you are not to worship them. Or, there are no other
gods and groveling before any of them will get the big guy just royally exer-
cised. I hope this clears it up. You don't choose your parents, do you?

It's like a river, see, you've got your main channel and your side streams, sand
bars, mud, bugs, towheads, that island where Huck and Jim hid out for days,
an old channel cat big as a pickup lurking in the deepest backwater. But every
river has banks, right? And nobody with the sense God gave turtles tries to
float the paddlewheel steamer up the flood plain. I hope you're getting this.

It's fine to wish for another God, one more like Einstein, say, or John Wooden,
or Mom. But watch out or you'll get what you ask for. What would you do
with a spirit in every tree, a quivering icon for every occasion, all of them
carping and making demands?

Believe me, you're jumbled and schizy enough already. Behave as if all this is
true and if not it won't matter, at least until much later, when the rains have
come, when the rolls on the counter have been toasted and eaten and the nap
on the couch left you calm as a parked car. In the good days God and country
were like those two peas, a sometimes awkward arrangement but gosh, we got
things done. First the anthem, then the invocation, then we played ball.

What should we salute now, with ten channels of the hard-eyed prophets shout-
ing that the victory is at hand? It's a gentle life. Pray every morning for grace
and wisdom, for release from your fears. At day's end you can ride the Metro
back from town, slide under the mean streets, sit on the deck in the dusk. Lift
the glass and mutter to the one who is smiling, saying nothing, there with you.

The Cookie Poem

"Here are my sad cookies."

The sad cookies. The once and future cookies.
The broken sweet cookies. The cookies
of heartbreaking beauty. The stony cookies
of Palestine. The gummy and delicious
olive and honey cookie. The pasty
damp cookie trapped in the child's hand.

Sad cookies, weird cookies, slippery
and dangerous cookies. Brilliant helpless
soiled and torn cookies, feverish and sweaty
cookies. Sullen cookies, sassy cookies,
the cookies of tantrum and the cookie of joy
and the sweet dark cookie of peace.

The faithful cookie of Rotterdam. The wild-eyed
cookie of Muenster. The salty Atlantic cookie.
Cookies in black coats, in coveralls,
in business suits, cookies in bonnets
and coverings and heels, cookies scratching
their heads and their bellies, cookies utterly
and shamelessly naked before the beloved.

Cookies of the Amish division, cookies
of the Wahlerhof, cookies of Zurich and
Strassburg and Volhynia and Chortitza,
Nairobi Djakarta Winnipeg Goshen.
Cookies who hand their children off
to strangers, who admonish their sons
to remember the Lord's Prayer, cookies
who say all right, baptize my children

and then sneak back to the hidden church anyway.
Cookies who cave in utterly. Cookies
who die with their boots on. Cookies
with fists, and with contusions.
The black hearted cookie. The cookie with issues.
Hard cookies, hot cookies, compassionate
conservative cookies, cookies we loathe
and love, cookies lost, fallen, stolen,
crushed, abandoned, shunned. Weary
and heroic cookies, scathingly noted cookies,
flawed cookies who did their best.
Single cookies, queer cookies, cookies of color,
homeless cookie families sleeping in the car,
obsolete cookies broken down on the information
highway. Sad cookies, silent cookies,
loud cookies, loved cookies, your cookies
my cookies our cookies, all cookies
God's cookies, strange sweet hapless cookies
marked each one by the Imago Dei,
oh the Father the Son the Mother the Daughter
and the Holy Ghost all love cookies,
love all cookies, God's mouth is full
of cookies, God chews and swallows and flings
hands wide in joy, the crumbs fly
everywhere, oh God loves us all.

How the Boy Jesus Resisted Taking Out the Trash

O there's not enough to bother with.
O in a couple thousand years the landfills will be groaning.
O we're too poor there isn't any trash.
O what about Naomi what does she do around here.
O if ever you suspected what's to come you'd put me in the best chair, you'd
        kill the last goat for supper and feed me the heart and the liver.
O not now.
O remember my father's business and all that. Priests and Levites are going
        to love me, some. Locusts will sing and sizzle. Precious stones will
        roll toward me like mice. Everybody's pretty daughters will cry
        because I don't like them that way.
O I'll change it into figs and honey later, all right?
O all right.

Ancient Themes #1: The Martyrs & the Child
-for di

this is really pretty cool isnt it
leaving it all out but the letters wow
it'll confuse my mom & piss off my teachers
so bad i always wanted to be bad or at least
i thought i was bad anyway i cant forget
those sunday school teachers
bernice for example my moms 1st cousin
there we all were in the church basement
i was 10 years old maybe & shes asking
if we are ready to die like the martyrs
get our tongues screwed & fingers splintered
get burned up like firewood to heat
the hearts of those left behind well
thats some question when youre 10
in the middle of america in 1962
already scared of dying aglow
with radiation never mind with zeal
for the lord so there i sat gulping
& stalling with only those flimsy
beige curtains between our class
& the others with only a floor & a ceiling
& several miles of sky between me
& god leaning down to listen
& then my cousin connie who later went
wild & beautiful said she would do it
she would die for jesus yes she would
& bernice seemed pleased & forgot to ask
the rest of us & so i blundered on
into the rest of my life sweating out
the nuke tests & the bullies & the wondrous
heedless girls treading the tender grass

of my stupid young heart & i was surely
not so much worse for being forced
into uneasy contemplation of the fiery
heroes of old of the godless commies
& whether indeed i was ready to go up
in pain & splendor for jesus for believers
baptism for dirk willems turning back
half crazed with love for his pursuer
half full of pious shit surely clear
full of some weird lust to leave
this world & head out on the ice not
the canal not the lake no the true crazy
buckling thin ocean of ice jesus laid down
behind on his way out of town follow me
follow me well are you coming or not

The Black Father

Not my real father still known as Whitey for his hair
for his open grin for his way of rubbing his head between
his work-thick hands when tired or embarrassed
but the father with secrets the black-haired father

the big smart father who learned to fly
who journeyed west & came home sad & triumphant
& filled with mysteries the black father agreed
to be the chosen one and he learned to speak in two voices

one used the old words few and strong the bible the vision
the stern & narrow way the other voice he kept
in his dark suit in an inside pocket held between chest
& arm too tight to slip out I guessed we guessed

at what wild secrets that voice knew we argued & proposed
but the suit stayed on the arm stayed down
the first voice kept talking it talked well
it had stories dramatic & perplexing

the last refugees pushed off the plane
the engines roaring to lift the groaning exiles
above the trees the father trembling at the stick
& we hushed & trembled & pondered what did that mean

while the father slipped away to answer one more
hard narrow letter about what some young fool
said on a weary Tuesday what some young body
did Saturday night on the gym floor

the black father didn't have it easy he gave

a lot up   he learned to choose his moments
& his fights & kept whole reams of careful argument
in his secret drawer for centuries

well years anyway   in my last year the black father
had the class over & I stood near him & tried to say
that he had taught me something I was twenty
& from the country & I faltered & for a second

he seemed ready to speak but then just looked
down & turned away   it was not his fault
I was shy & young   bold only at the wrong moments
& maybe he was shy too but oh black father

I want to know what it was you almost said
what that inside pocket held & why you turned away

Valley, Old Man, Paper Cup

Say the whole valley shimmered
under half an inch of dingy water.
Say you tried to climb a big rock

slipped back and gave up. Say
you tried to come out safe or true
or clever. Later would you find yourself

climbing the hill just to warm your hands?
When the bell clanged for supper
would you turn back right away?

This is the rock where the copperhead bit.
This, where the river runs in flood.
The sky pressed flat as tinfoil,

charcoal trees, scant leaves trembling
in the cold. Violet, may-apple,
you slip twice but don't fall

on the quivery rocks laid to cross
the riffle of water. On the far side
sprays of blossom gaud the side hill,

two hawks wheel, the clouds shred themselves.
In the small flat field you pitch
the elegant tent, flaps knuckling

in the wind. Yes it will make you happy.
Yes it will make you good. Yes an old man
will hand you his cup and you will pour

it full and put it back into his hand.

4.

Letter to J. from the Ramada Inn Western Avenue, Albany

Here's what I think: God wants us all
to love each other, but even God is not
sure how. We're still more in the dark,
so as you always say it's hard. We have
to learn how to be friends, true and mostly
apart, entangled with all our various others.
But today I'm bent toward sentiment and hoping
for indulgence as I offer thanks for having
taught me all that stuff I thought I knew
just wasn't so. I've tried to listen.
I've watched you flip your hair back—
like a soft cape, hunch and get me
with those eyes and say OK, here's the thing.

And there are lots of things. In Albany
the hard spring project is underway.
I crossed the highway to the campus,
took the path around the pond, new leaves
hesitating out, crunch of my shoes
on the path, each step easier. I'd been
inside too long. A charming woman
with a terrier smiled and tugged
the leash. A crow vectored this way,
another that way. The signs pointed
to Colonial, State, Freedom.

I asked if all your other male friends
were gay and you laughed and said, mostly,
swinging down the street. As if.
You know how it is, saying things that
are more or less true and also way wrong?
It's my main talent, some days.

So how do we get from colonial to freedom?
Is there talk that's also action, words
to change the world? My father never talks
to women who aren't relatives or married
to him. Most of the people I can talk to
are women, most of them married to someone else.
From the fifth floor of the Ramada
the view is clear but mixed, yellowy
streamers of a big weeping willow,
shabby balconies of the Capitol
(from $39.00) Lodge. Everybody's gone
but me, I took this late flight back
saying it was cheap but secretly
wanting this six hours alone and free
to be silent and selfish, to choose
my own steps.
        One window's almost
clear, the other etched and streaky.
Three flags—US, Canada, Ramada—
keep trying to find some accommodation
with the wind. I could drink the whisky
I didn't drink with the boys last night
but I'd rather have coffee. This is taking
longer than I thought. I always want
to think things aren't so bad, you always
want to fix them.
        You taught me that
I trust myself too much, you made me listen,
talk wise and dense as cherry or mahogany.
You can't drive nails through such wood
and finally I laid my hammer down, though
it's still in the toolbox.

So here I am, stalling, tinkering, waiting
for some body to start muttering in my left ear.
This is all about me. You have no truck
with this mushy mystic stuff, when I show you
the poems I don't get but can't abandon
you don't get them either. It's all just
spiderweb and guesswork and semi-truths anyway.
All of your male friends are gay. All
of my women friends are secretive luminous
and troubled, they talk all the time
and teach me incredible things but only
very slowly, I forget the simplest ones over
and over. Even this is wrong. Especially
this. At best a few of my opinions
have blown over in the big storms like poplars
or Chinese elms, fast-growing but flimsy.
The hard oaks and maples are still scrubby
and weak, inching their way toward heaven.

There are lots of things, few of them pure,
many of them good. It's no easier
for me to quit figuring where I stand
than for you to quit wondering how
your hair looks. How hard to move rightly,
to avoid the old tracks. Three times
I found myself on the same path around
the pond, scenic but not getting me
any closer to home. How many times
have I made that old round through desire
and propriety. How hard to say things straight.
Nothing that is said clearly can be
said truly about the gods wrote that old
pantheist C. S. Lewis. How little
we know and how much we get wrong.

There's space for many loves in any heart
if we learn to let them in and out,
to roll and carry them like shirts,
like books we buy and haul back home,
heavy but precious, dense and dangerous
as radium, the pages whispering in
the whistly dark of the baggage hold,
six miles above the ground, swift and
precarious as anything that must be owned
and shared at the same time. God wants
us all to love each other. But only
very slowly can we teach each other how.

5.

Driving with Rumi

So let us not be sure of anything,
only ourselves, only that,
so that miraculous beings
can come running to help.
       -Maulana Jalal al-Din Rumi

I've been talking into this little box with it stuck on pause. But now here I am, going where I'm led by the roads and the signs and the map, trying to stay in my lane and in the clear, trying to drive a little too fast without getting punished, trying to pass some of the traffic and let the rest pass me.

And I have Rumi on the tape player, with spacy Eastern music behind, Coleman Barks' wild southern drawl chanting the secret lines. I've been watching the human stuff go by, road and ditch and overpass and cars, buildings on one side and trucks on the other, how thick it is everywhere. And I've been wishing for some place beyond, behind, above all this, some place pure and true and real, some place before the human world.

A good way back I passed a field of waist-high brush, brownish scrub weeds and wildflowers, and as I zipped by enclosed in the car I had a quick impulse to go hide there, find a place where I could crawl in and take cover. I know how sentimental that is, how unlikely, but it still went through my head.

And Rumi says this:

But I feel more like a flute
that you put into your mouth
and then neglect to blow.

And I shut the tape off and let that one settle in the stillness for a while as I go down the road and past a broken-down truck with orange triangles out to warn the rest of us, and another truck driver eases toward my lane to give it some space as he passes, but I'm here, he can't go too far. He just has to ease out toward the white line, and I ease out toward the yellow line and we ease on, making our little adjustments, waiting for some wind to blow on our flutes.

And Rumi says this:

No one knows what makes the soul
wake up so happy. Maybe a dawn breeze
is blowing the veil from the face of God.

And I don't know what's in my left eye that's making me blink and rub it and blink again thinking if I just irritate it enough it'll come clean. I know if you want to feel how small you are there's nothing like getting in a car by yourself and driving across the world for a little while, learning again how long it takes to get anywhere, how far apart the real things are, how tiny your place in the mind of God must be.

All morning I fussed and stewed on the broken machines I own, how much time and money they will cost to fix. Now I'm riding in one that's not broken, going as fast as I can, my hands a little tired on the steering wheel but I'm going down the road, wheeling toward Wheeling. Oh, it's a gorgeous world and the sun's going down and the golden November light falls sideways on everything, the big flatbed semi loaded with the barky slices left from cutting lumber out of trees, skins bound off to be firewood or pulp, pieces hanging off everywhere, a big slab nearly in my face as I peel quickly into the left lane to get by, to get ahead, where it can't fall on me.

And Rumi says this:

Birds make great white sky circles
of their freedom. How do they learn it?
They fall. And falling, they are given wings.

And plenty of things are circling and falling and whirling, the music whirls, the engine whirls, the pistons and crankshaft, the oil and the antifreeze are whirling and the blood in my body is whirling, my head is whirling as the neurons fire and relax, spark and wink. As for me I'm holding steady, I'm holding the wheel and I'm staying in my lane and I'm getting ready to cross the bridge to West Virginia, to the next state, I see the blue metal girders arching like some coil reaching out of me, out across the water, touching down, touching something bigger, something older, something else.

[Quotes are from *Rumi: The Voice of Longing* by Coleman Barks]

Jacob's Creek

It runs louder even than the turnpike,
making its own business. Should I put
my fingers in? And where? The rocks

are slick and mossy, I'll be drenched,
embarrassed, late. Anyhow I know
the feel of water. I know a lot of things,

not to write a lot as one word,
not to worry much about the sleep
I've lost. I know to hang back, let

the moment's rush and churn fill the page
almost without me. The water is cold,
not clear but smooth and moving fast.

Upstream it parts around a little island
where a few drenched trees hold steady
and shape their simple loud thoughts

to fit the curves and edges of a hard
and wet and roaring world, a strong
and gray and green and airy world,

the world where the fisher dips his bait
and hook and leader, lets the current
draw them, lifts and lowers them again.

Things of No Use in the Morning

No use to wonder will it rain more,
or to stop at the rain-splash
glazing every leaf and rock. No use

to worry that this trail might not go
to Sunset Hill at all. No use to squint
at the spiderweb of rope, the tires,

the V of cable strung among the trees.
No use to stop at the limb that fell
across the path, a door left open

just a crack, or where the soaked
branches sag into the trail, or at
the little waterslip where you must

jump and slide and wet one shoe.
No use to sit on the mossy rock
until the water soaks through.

Just stand in the bird-sweet
morning air. Let the small bugs
and mosquitoes prowl, rhododendrons

and black maples stretch into
their morning bath of sunlight.
Wind will stir the leaves,

and big drops spatter like
the afterthoughts of God:
This is just practice.
Soon everything will shine.

Shelter

The world is stony but large.
It holds many quiet things.
A tiny refuge, green or yellow,

is enough. A soul could hide
in the corkscrew willow,
in the yellow butterfly.

A soul could hide
in the wine-dark geranium
or the space behind the cricket's leg

if it knew how long, no,
never mind how long, if it
only knew some day for sure.

What the Boy Knows

> "There's a boy in you about three
> Years old . . ."
> —Robert Bly, "One Source of Bad Information"

When nothing is working, hit something hard.

Or just yell.

Except for Mom, girls are stupid.

The only good rocks are small enough to throw.

Books are stupid, cats are stupid, dishes are stupid.

Turtles are cool. Ants are cool. Fire is cool.

Flat rocks will skip but not all of them.

The only way to tell is to throw them all.

The best thing is playing in the mud with a stick.

We need a big dog that hates everyone but us.

Not too big a stick.

The more the dog barks the braver we'll be.

What the Old Guy Says

Ignorance will get you somewhere, but you won't like it.

If the water is way down it makes a new shore.

No matter what the signs say, somebody
will nail a new cleat to the tree.

That thing the waves do? It's a word.

A good rope can hang a long time and still be ready.

You think you know your name, and all the time
the world is sliding through your mouth.

God made the water so you'd realize you're not in charge.

The longer the first skip, the shorter the rest.

It's dark down there and cold, but not dead.

What the Prairie Boy Learned on the Whistler Road

In mountains there's only one way home. Drive
or let somebody else. In mountains all deliberations
end in aesthetics or triage.

In mountains you don't need faith to believe that God
is both sublime and funky. Phrases like inscrutable workmanship
make sense. Of course, you say, souls can be washed clean.

At this coast the islands are mountains with wet feet,
their heads dizzy in the late haze. They get up early
but laze through the day, sure there's another coming.

In mountains a blue-black rock loomed in its fogs,
dire and high-toned as a desert prophet. One glimpse,
all I could spare, then back to the cars, the signs, the next curve.

It was enough. Where I live there are no mountains. Lack
is the father of beauty. Beauty is the father of the mountains.
The mountains are the father of everything.

Crow

-Millersville, 1995

The women have been talking of their silences, their losses, their long walks and bruises. Trying to write a bridge between the sides of the split self. Winding up with a volcano.

When in doubt just say oh, or one of those leaning words The one who hears the true song shall surely die. How does a conscientious objector find his inner warrior, he asks, and everybody titters.

The women have been speaking well, standing up to thank each other. I ran this morning in the old streets of Millersville, all by myself except for three crows in a vacant lot like soldiers on patrol, walking, glaring, waiting.

What is structure, what is agency? Outside and inside? Even given primogeniture and eons of patriarchy, who can say the men ever managed to make anything go just their way?

You can play within the rules, or play with the rules, but it's hard to play without them. Eva Wagler was either a lush and temptress who needed a firm hand, or another hapless victim of the men. The records are unclear.

Crows in the field a dark and glossy black, private and strong and no threat to me. And then why did I see them as old men, why did they frighten me so?

In Lancaster County there are so many Amish women working at their own little businesses that Amish house cleaning services have sprung up, Amish gardening and canning services.

And the crows are there in the middle, indifferent, pacing. They cackle and flap. Can they be happy?

The liaison between a nice Menno girl from Ohio and postmodern theory. Knotting together history, identity, God. Can you live in two worlds if you're not ashamed of either? Let's be honest instead of good. Let's dance outside the wall, wild as we know.

The crows tell long obscure stories but only in the barn and the fields. The crows preach every other Sunday in the cave in the woods. They don't care if the women gather to discuss the symbology of red, how they survived, who did the work.

The crows share out the vacant lot among themselves, there's only just enough, they don't care if the crows down the block are starving.

They walk carefully, their eyes fully open, who knows what's coming in the next second. They are wary of the sick glow of nostalgia. They know just filling in the gaps is not enough. They know how shaky and defenseless the light is, that if they don't stare hard and sharp enough everything will vanish.

Is that a woman crow? Is that a husband crow? A crow whose gender is guiltily constructed? We all want to restore our heart's desire, to have it included, to have it named.

The crows aren't hunting food, they're hunting for the forest they remember, the nest they left in 1643. Right here, they say, it was right here, and walk and stare and poke their hard beaks into the empty air.

That was the end, I thought. But the crows aren't done with me, they leap and flap away, they circle in the winds inside my head, they tear at the walls with claws and beaks. You think, they scream, you think you've got us?

Crows in the air. One crow in the air, calling. Three colts running, rearing in a pasture, flailing at each other with their half-grown hooves. Six crows in a clutch on the mountain, wheeling. Crow probing the litter at the side of the road. Crow in the median, then black tire scraps.

Life Study with Obstinate Questionings, or the Sweat Bee

The world's grown half over and through
the steel buildings. It's slowly taking back
the pile of debris from the old house in town,

the one we half-burned and half-buried
hoping nobody would notice. One wet spring
and the world is half over all our paths,

green enough to hide a horde of mayflies,
beetles, mosquitoes, on and on. The world
is red clover, milkweed, goldenrod, foxtail,

this loose and inept catalogue could go on.
If I were in charge I'd lose the flies
first thing, I'd keep the dragonflies and

whatever didn't bite through my socks or whine
in my ear. God knows his own. But now I think
God is a catbird, poised on a limb as I am

on the fence, balanced but not quite easy,
trying to sing. Unless God is the swallow
blazing past almost too sudden to see,

savoring deft wings and sharp beak and the soft
delicious bugs. Unless God is the muskrat,
dazed and easy in the slippery mud. Unless

I'm a fool, and God is elsewhere, out, beyond,
behind, and all the bushes hide is dirt,
and even the new bird singing so firm and clean

is only bird, and the ones that answer too.
I'm a fool but I think God is the fat groundhog
that hunched off through the grass, the goldfinch

that skipped into the fine web of leaves
and branches, the sweat bee that followed me
half the way home, trying to nest in my hair.

On the Western Slope

"Damballah Wedo is . . . the great father of whom one asks
    nothing save his blessing."
        -Maya Deren, *Divine Horsemen: The Voodoo Gods of Haiti*

That week the old mountain came back, floated grand and nonchalant above
the valley. They looked but mostly didn't, pointed the car this way, that way,
ate and argued, slept. Clouds clotted, melted off before noon. They sang
Our god is an awesome god, as though they had him surrounded and could
explain. But he was cross and sleepy when the woman turned up, pale and
nearly naked, walking gently toward the mountain.

When she waved from the mists he stared, eyes and feet heavy, heavy, though
the coffee basked in the sun near his hand. She raised an arm again and he
thought, How did I sleep so long? He got up, humming. The streets hung
clean and straight, the poplar quivered, the paving stones glowed like tablets
fallen from the mountain.

He picked up a fist-sized black stone with one ragged edge. Primitive chop-
ping stone, he thought, then felt silly. The next rooms were empty, but then
at last the altar, the cup. He struck a pose, smiled. Wild laughter from the
shadows. Then Mum called them to supper.

His head still hurt. When he opened the pack, it held only the black stone.
His sons laughed, bitterly. He weighed it in his hand, where it felt heavy,
heavy, but somehow right. The youngest threw it out the door, and it broke
exactly in two.

Grass

What is this craving, like wind
through the clothesline pole
in the midst of the ordinary day?
I know what I want: to be better,

more, less. I know the verse
on the image of God. I know where
a river begins as a waterway
sown to grass, and last week

my father drove me slowly down it,
the blue pickup bouncing over
a thousand stubborn clumps
and the tiny washouts between them.

This spring he found two boys
in a weedy draw, smoking,
a quarter mile from the road.
He slowed the mower, yelled,

"Watch out for snakes!"
Today I paid twenty bucks
for two hours, a lifetime,
of music. Goodman is dead

of the cancer, stubby fingers
gone to bone. But he left
the song about the con man,
the real gold is inside us all,

his voice so full of loss
and laughter that you can't tell

where the irony starts and ends.
I bet he didn't know himself,

like me. It's hard to get clear
inside the rooms and streets
of this town, a cool summer night,
the bugs in soft clouds

at the screens. The wine
is gone, the game is over.
The mown ends of the grass
learn their slow way back

to the soil. The old news
lies yellow and brittle
under a bush, ready to crumble
and blow off to paradise.

Right Here, or The Realist Aesthetic

We like to live this way. We get along.
Our serious birdwatchers live a block over,
next to the fiend for antique cars. Sports fans

are everywhere, like the geese. The lyric
of our place and time runs bland and various
as the Little Riley Creek, almost clear right now,

tan with mud and flood two weeks ago, bare stone
in the dry months. It all depends on the rain.
We don't get to choose. No smoky ruins here,

no crack or switchblades in sight, no cosmic battles
by the soccer fields. We speak plain, as if we
can understand each other, as if it matters.

I could capture the chickadee with my bare hand,
or claim I did. A river of blood could run
like a supple leopard from the victim's body

to the feet of his mother, curling and whining
for attention. Oh sure, say my people. Me too.
That's all feet and feathers and it's vegetarian

lasagna we need, and red meat we want. In my town
the Lions have eaten watery ham and boiled green beans
since the fifties. They're changed but alive.

Myself these days I'm hanging wallpaper, avoiding
most conversation. We're all waiting for the new slide
to open at the pool. We all need a thrill. Last night

I thought I awoke and heard my wife sighing,
but she said nothing. Then I seemed to remember
waking other nights and hearing her, restless,

and not knowing if she really was awake, whether
I should speak, or touch her, or keep quiet.
I touched her hip. The night was still. We slept.

White River

The red gravel dipping and weaving brokenly through trees
reminded me of other roads I know that lead to rivers
in Colorado, Illinois, but this was Arkansas and the White River,

fast moving, high, surprisingly clear though not truly white.
Two men and a woman in a small motorboat waved and didn't stop
until I waved back. Their wake wet my shoes.

Above the other bank two crows harried a very big hawk.
And a man was near me suddenly on the boat slip, asking
if the river'd gone down, and I said it's high but I don't know

how high it's been. We talked a little, agreed it was cooler
on the bank, he told me that he used to swim here, but now
with the North Fork dam and the water coming off the bottom

it's too cold. It would stagger a man. I'll leave you alone,
he said, I just came to see how the river was doing.
The river was calming since the boat had gone by,

and there were crows and what might have been an ovenbird
and one tree above all the rest, sparsely leaved but spread
with yellow blossoms, gorgeous even clear across the river.

Since I don't need to deck this river out for summer, since it
only wants a channel and some rock beneath, since I need this river
more than it needs me, I touched it—not cold near shore, almost clear.

I waited there beside it for the short time I had. I listened
and watched for the birds. If the river told me anything
I wouldn't hold it back. But it didn't say anything in words.

Landscape with Daily Life

"God is not big, he is right."
                    -William Stafford

Thistle. Milkweed. Grasses
already seeding. Rapid wings.
Geese on the island, geese in
the water. At the edge, the grass
climbs six feet or more. What would
change if I knew the true name
of anything I see? Brushing past
I loosen the seeds, carry them
with me. I don't mind all this
listening and looking, even when
it's only the world. I can breathe
deep or shallow, I can leave
when I choose. I'm not milkweed
or thistle or three-leaf ivy
though like them I live my other,
daily life. Now here we are.
The thistles don't care. The grass
tries one way, then another,
then just stays. I can't help
it, I love this place. I leave.
Tonight we will sleep in the old
new world, in the daily bed,
trees breathing near the window,
the two of us inside, steady
in the tall, sweet grass.

Jeff Gundy's earlier books include *Inquiries* (Botttom Dog) and *Flatlands* (Cleveland State), poems, and *A Community of Memory: My Days with George and Clara* (Illinois), creative nonfiction. He has been awarded Ohio Arts Council Fellowships for Poetry. Raised in central Illinois, he studied at Goshen College and Indiana University, and since 1984 has taught at Bluffton College in Ohio. He and his wife Marlyce have three sons. His most cherished possessions are a slightly battered 1963 Martin D- guitar—a family heirloom—and a new Taylor 12-string.